Vol 15

MAZE

Ages 4-6

FOR KIDS

MAZE BOOK

f /MySweetBooks1

/MySweetBooks1

/MySweetBooks1

/MySweetBooks

Email Us : mysweetbooks1@gmail.com

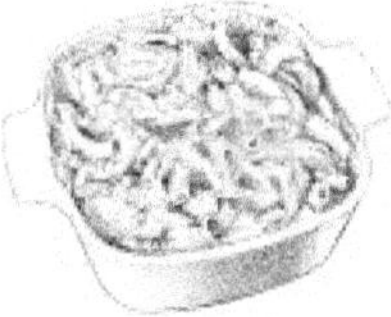

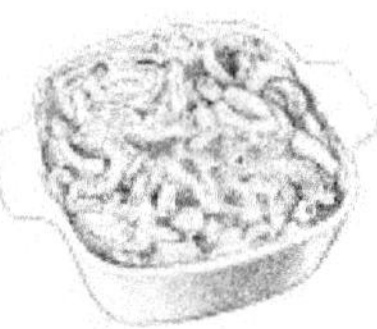

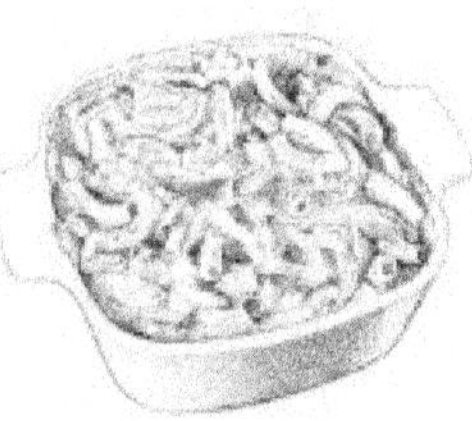

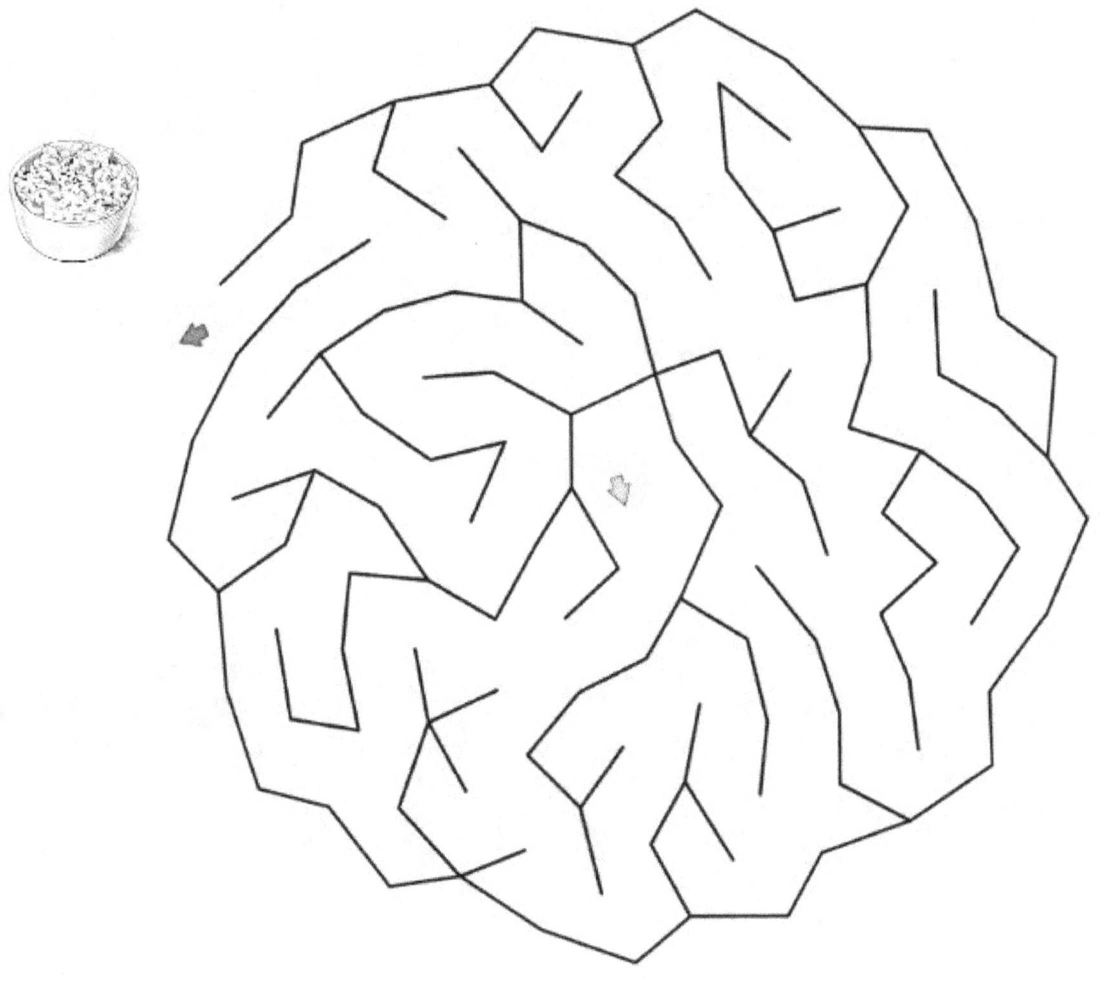

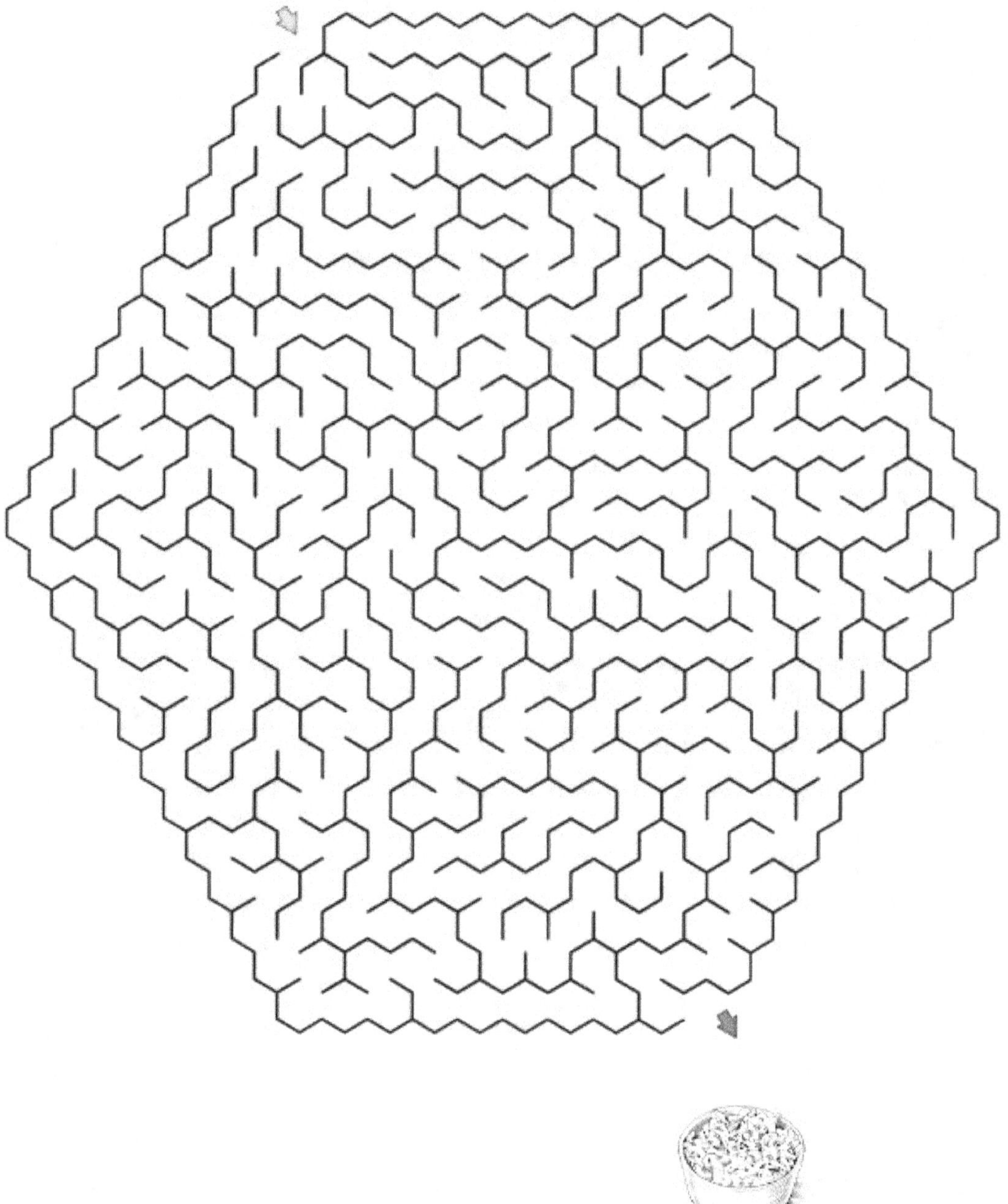

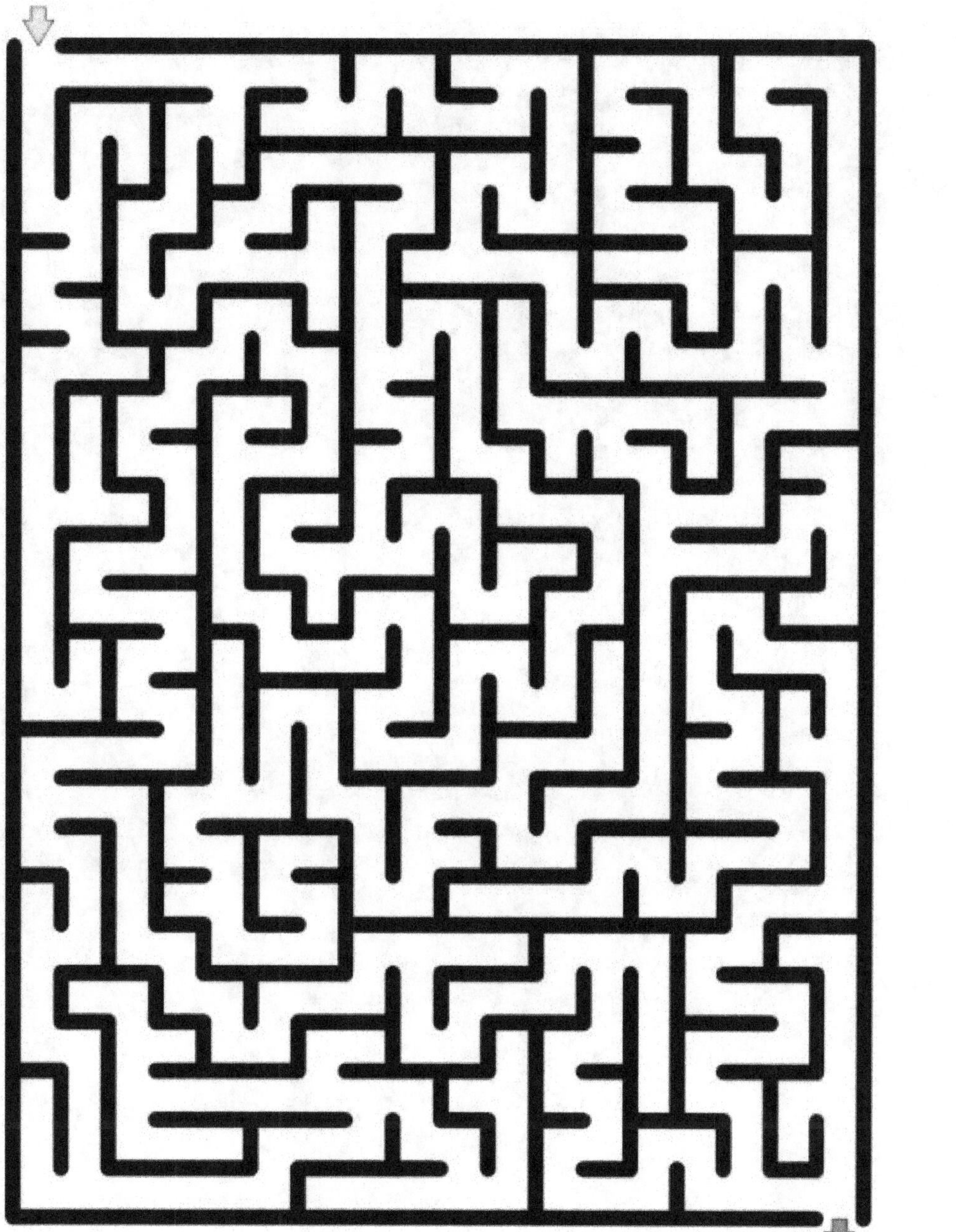

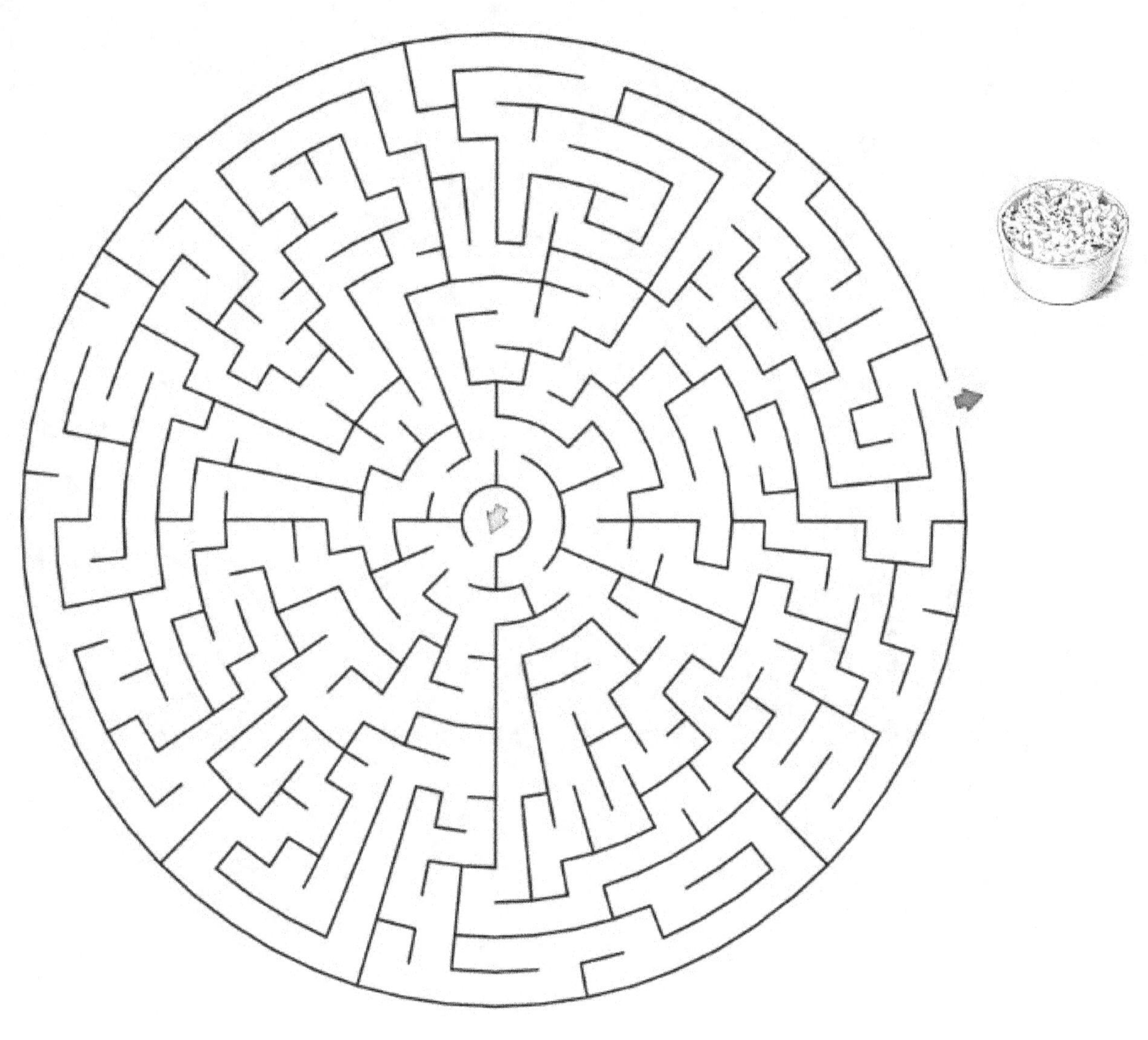

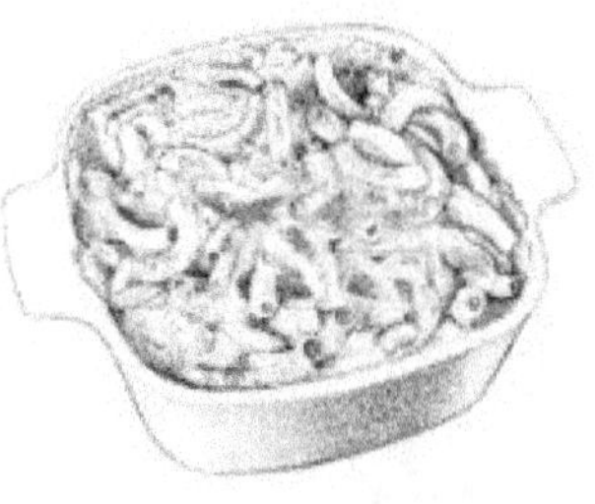

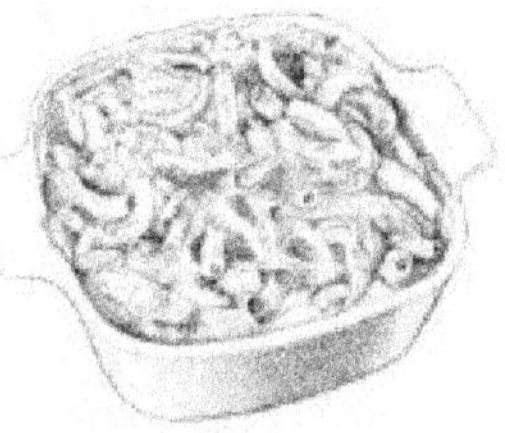

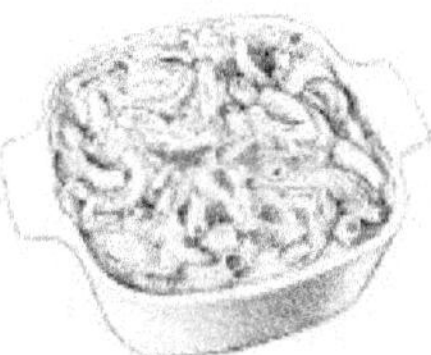

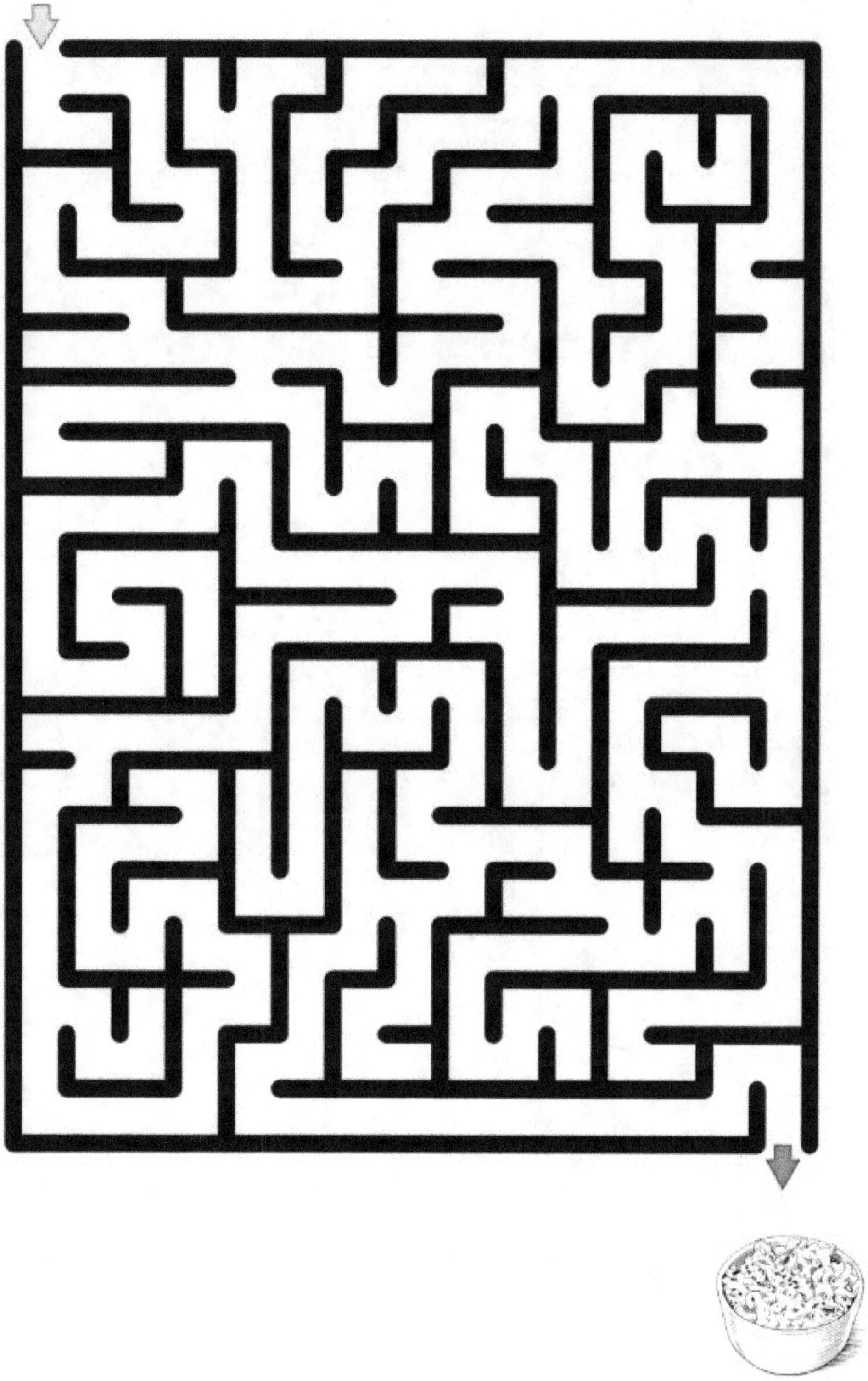